Feng Shui for Teens

Feng Shui for Teens

◆

An easy-to-read guide for teens to learn Feng Shui with tips on how to create fun and fabulous rooms

DeAnna Radaj

iUniverse, Inc.
New York Lincoln Shanghai

Feng Shui for Teens
An easy-to-read guide for teens to learn Feng Shui with tips on how to create fun and fabulous rooms

iUniverse books may be ordered through booksellers or by contacting:

iUniverse
2021 Pine Lake Road, Suite 100
Lincoln, NE 68512
www.iuniverse.com
1-800-Authors (1-800-288-4677)

The views expressed in this work are solely those of the author and do not necessarily reflect the views of the publisher, and the publisher hereby disclaims any responsibility for them.

ISBN: 978-0-595-42873-1 (pbk)
ISBN: 978-0-595-87212-1 (ebk)

Printed in the United States of America

To Kate, you were such a help and very supportive in this endeavor! You are a talented and creative person with a lot to offer! Thank you for all of your input in this project.

To Sherry.... or rather Cheri.... ha ha.... I promised you I would make amends on the 2ⁿᵈ book! Thanks for your positive-ness and for being a great sounding board and "vent-ee."

To the usual cast of characters: Deb, Nancy, Renee, Cristina and Marg. Your continued support and friendship means the world to me. Thank you.

To all of my clients and workshop attendees, you keep me on top of my game and striving to learn more. Thank you for the motivation.

To my Mom, your continued belief in me means the world to me!

Contents

Introduction
So What's the Deal w/this Feng Shui?

Funky shoes? Funk schway? What? You've all heard of feng shui (pronounced fung shway), the Chinese art of placement, but did you know that it has been around for over 5000 years? Feng shui has gained popularity in the USA in the past 15 years, and interior designers, architects and real estate agents nation-wide are using its principles. At its most basic level, feng shui is about living in harmony with your surrounding environment. Its concepts include gaining an understanding of the five elements (Fire, Water, Earth, Metal and Wood), color theory and its affects on your physical and mental health and living WITH your environment rather than bulldozing through it.

Bedrooms for children and teens can be challenging for even the most experienced designer, as these spaces are used for a variety of reasons: sleeping, studying, entertaining, dreaming, watching TV and playing video games. This book will teach you some basic feng shui principles for the Black Hat Sect school, which will be explained in further detail in a later chapter, the proper use of color and accessories, the importance of engaging all of your senses and how to apply them in your VIS (very important space). By learning these techniques, you will be able to apply the principles to any space and watch all the positive changes that will occur in your life, while your friends ask you how you did it.

You will also do some soul-searching regarding what is important in your life (goals and priorities) as you become familiar with the 9 life areas (Career/Life Aspirations, Knowledge/Spirituality, Family, Wealth/Abundance, Success/Fame/ Luck, Relationships, Creativity/Kids, Travel/Helpful People and Health/Well-Being) that are illustrated by the Bagua (pronounced bah-gwa) board. As you work with these areas and learn when to tweak an area of interest, you will notice the positive affect feng shui will have on your life and relationships with others.

Using the Bagua board will become ingrained after awhile, and you will be able to walk into any space and know if one of your friends is having homework problems by the state of their Knowledge area or notice if the Relationship area is out of whack by the big piles of dirty laundry in that area. Feng shui principles will also help you identify the "whys" of things being unbalanced and "how" to make corrections.

The effect your stuff has on your well being, physical and mental, is discussed in (at) great length. From a feng shui standpoint, you will see that where your clutter is piled-up is probably a life area that you are also having issues with (or at the very least needs some TLC). You will also start to take particular notice of your collections and other belongings and learn what they say about you. You will realize the importance of looking forward and reaching higher to achieve your dreams, how to let go and not cling to items from the past (which can harbor negative or bad feelings) and not carry around this emotional baggage throughout your life.

Don't know how to get started on your journey? Need some help defining your priorities and goals? Well, after many years of study, teaching and consulting on numerous interior design projects, and much research, this book was compiled to help you take control of your life, set the course for your future and design the life of your dreams. Here are some quick tips to help you get started:

- Be fearless. Great change requires you to actually make a great change. This can be moving your bed to a different part of the room, painting a wall a different color, driving a different route to school or sitting in a different part of the lunchroom. You get the idea. It can be scary at first, however, none of these changes are permanent, and the affects can be life changing. You could meet a new friend, sleep better at night or find a shortcut to your favorite coffee shop!

- Think out of the box in applying feng shui to your space. Feng shui can be personalized to what makes you unique! If you want to work on your KNOWLEDGE area, which suggests you add the color BLUE, but you have a pink and green room and a blue wall won't cut it, you could use blue bookmarks for your books or get a blue mouse pad for your computer. Remember, the changes you make don't have to be on a massive scale, just something different to remind you of your new intention.

- Trust your gut. If something doesn't feel right, don't do it, even if directed to in a book or by a friend or family member. Trust your own intuition in finding the right arrangement that works for you. However, as stated before, change can be scary. Try to live with the change for at least a day or two, as fear of taking control of your space and life can be overwhelming. If it still doesn't feel right, try something else. Change is scary, but it can also be fun as you watch all of the new things that start to occur.

- Most importantly, have FUN as you make new choices and start taking control of the direction of your life. When working through this book play your favorite music, speak in an accent or wear "feng shui clothes" when you are making these changes. Have fun, be crazy and creative, and enjoy the process.

Are you ready to begin?...

Chapter 2
The (Abridged) History of Feng Shui

Feng shui is the Chinese tradition that focuses on living in harmony with your environment (home or school). Basically, feng shui is how you interact with your surroundings through your furniture arrangement, color scheme and accessories and collections choices. These choices can either block or improve your energy (chi). When the energy in your space flows freely life is fabulous, things get finished on time, you feel happy and eager to learn new things about yourself. However, when your energy is blocked you feel overwhelmed, unhappy and drained.

***Chi is the cosmic, universal energy that flows around us and through our spaces, and influences our lives. Feng shui uses color, the five senses, the five elements and accessories to manipulate chi so it flows freely throughout a space. ***

Literally translated, feng shui means "wind and water." Feng shui was actually started as a way to identify or select auspicious (ideal/positive) gravesites in China over 5,000 years ago. It was thought that the better the position of the gravesite, the better the fortunes of the remaining family members. Many schools of thought have surfaced over the years. It is because of this that there is so much confusion. What direction should the door face? Where is the relationship area? Where do I put a crystal? No mirrors in the bedroom? Ahhhhhhh!

First and foremost, knowing which school you are dealing with and whether you are comfortable with that philosophy will make the biggest difference when designing your space. Once you know that, you are ready to begin. It should be noted that the following are very brief descriptions of the various schools.

The first school of thought, and considered to be the oldest, is the **Form** school. The Form school takes into consideration all geographical formations in and around the area where a building is being built. A great example is the "armchair" analogy. The best place to build is in the "seat" of the chair. The area behind the building should be as high or higher than your home, like a backrest. This can be accomplished with tree placement, or the house behind you is as big as or bigger than yours. This is a psychologically secure position. The building to each side are the "armrests" and should be no higher than your building and ideally a little smaller. This is for protection on each side as well. The front of the space should be clear and clutter-free, and nothing higher than 5' as you want to be able to see anyone approaching. There should be no large obstructions blocking your view-this includes trees, fences or other buildings (i.e. garage, shed, etc ...)

The next school is the **Compass** school. This is the school most thought of when feng shui is mentioned. Picture an old Chinese man with a compass pointing in various directions. This compass can identify where your bed should go and on what diagonal the desk should be placed. This school uses a compass called a Lo-pan to correctly determine the degree of the direction that is the most auspicious, or best, location for a particular room or piece of furniture. There are various calculations that are used in this school that are based on the date of birth of the occupants and the "birth" (can be construction date or date you moved in) of the house. Based on these calculations, you can derive your personal auspicious numbers or "pa-kua" numbers. These numbers relate to the directions in an "auspicious" (positive) or "inauspicious" (negative) way. The basis or principle here is to take advantage of or maximize your good/positive directions. You can take advantage of your auspicious/good directions by facing them, while keeping your back to inauspicious/bad directions.

Finally, there is the **Black Hat Sect** school of thought or **Bagua School**. (This is the school that is the basis of this book). Bagua is a Chinese word that translated means an "8-sided figure" or octagon shaped. This figure is then divided into segments, like a pie, with a center piece-giving you nine areas. Think of a tic-tac-toe board. These nine areas are then assigned names, colors, shapes and an element that corresponds to an assigned life area. The nine life areas of the Bagua are: Career/Life Path, Knowledge/Spirituality, Family, Wealth/Abundance, Success/Fame/Luck, Relationships, Creativity/Kids, Helpful People/Travel, and Health/Well-Being. The Bagua board can be used to space plan, accessorize and plan the color scheme of a home, room, desk, classroom, lunchroom, bed or garden.

In using and applying the Bagua board to your space, you must line up the bottom row (Knowledge/Spirituality, Career/Life Path and Helpful People/Travel) with the entryway wall of the room. So, first you must draw the floor plan of your room or "bird's eye view," including the doorway and windows, and then plot/ draw the corresponding life areas around the perimeter. Still a little confused? Stand in the entryway of your room and look INTO the space. If the door/entry is in the LEFT corner looking in, you enter the room from the Knowledge/Spirituality area. If you enter the room from the CENTER of the entryway wall, you enter the room from the Career/Life Path area. Lastly, if you enter the room from the RIGHT corner, you enter the room from the Helpful People/Travel area. This should help you in plotting out the rest of the room. Then you can superimpose the Bagua over the floor plan and see what "areas" need to be worked on, or what areas you'd like to work on. You will analyze furniture placement, accessories and/or piles of clutter. Once you get the concept of the Bagua and how to properly line up the grid, you will be able to work on any space and be able to identify the corresponding life area. See below:

Wealth/Abundance	Success/Fame	Relationships
Purple/Metallic	Red	Red/Pink/Peach
Water Element	Fire Element	Earth Element
Wavy lines	Triangle	Squares
SE	S	SW
Family	**Health/Well-Being**	**Creativity/Kids**
Green	Yellow/Earth-tones	White/Metallic
Wood Element	Earth Element	Metal Element
Rectangle	Squares	Circles
E	Center	W
Knowledge/Spirituality	**Career/Life Path**	**Helpful People/Travel**
Blue	Black	Gray
Earth Element	Water Element	Metal Element
Squares	Wavy Lines	Circles
NE	N	NW

Now that you have the Bagua board plotted out on your floor plan, you can "activate" these areas by using the element, color, shape, personal item or direction that is associated with that particular life area. An example of this is a pink stone heart in the Relationships area or a coin dish placed in the Wealth/Abundance area.

Use the following table to help you define your goals. Rank each life area from 1-9 with 1 being the most important and 9 being the least important area of concern in your life. Then write down notes to help define your goals.

Life Area	Rank	Goals
Career/Life Path		
Knowledge/Self-Empowerment/Spirituality		
Family		
Wealth/Abundance		
Success/Fame/Luck		
Relationships		
Creativity/Kids		
Helpful People/Travel		

Health/Well-Being

EX: If you ranked the Knowledge area as #1 area to work on, your goals would be

- Study an extra hour a week
- Keep desk clutter-free and stocked with only items essential to studying. homework and on-going school projects.

OK—ready to start living the life of your dreams? Here are the three main tips for you to use to help you begin:

1. Think objectively about your family, friends, places and goals you have in your life. Are you happy with the state of your relationships? Would you like to improve your social life? Would you like to go to a college out of state? Is your space cluttered and chaotic? Write down what you'd like to achieve and accomplish in your relationships and life.

2. The next step is to clear the clutter-mental and physical. Clutter is defined as ANYTHING that lowers your energy (i.e. do you feel angry, sad, depressed when you look at an item?). If you don't love it-get rid of it.

3. Now, use the Bagua board and the rest of the tips in this book to rearrange your space. Then sit back and see the positive changes that occur and how wonderful you feel as you take charge of your life!

Now let's begin …

Chapter 3
The Bagua Board

The Bagua board is one of the coolest (and easiest) tools to use in setting up your feng shui-ed room. Bagua is pronounced as "ba-GWA," and is the chart you use to show where the nine life areas are located in any space. Once your room is mapped out, you can then rearrange it, add color and/or accessories to activate the chi/energy you are trying to create in that area.

If you have questions about the use of the Bagua board, take a few minutes and review the previous chapter. Then stand in the room to be mapped out and turn the Bagua so that the bottom three sections (Knowledge, Career, Helpful People/ Travel) are aligned with the doorway wall. If it helps, write down the color, element and accessories to remind you what you can use to activate a selected area. Mapping out the space will help you to visualize the nine life areas and to see what is missing in your life and how to bring it into your life.

*** It should be noted that a bright light could work in any of the life areas to "shine light" on a particular area. ***

Here is a quick questionnaire to help you set your personal goals and priorities, and to see which life areas you may need to focus on. Circle the applicable answer after each question. Be honest in your answers!

1. Do you know what you are going to major in at college and pursue as a career?   Y   N

2. Do you often feel anxious or stressed?   Y   N

3. Do you frequently have earaches or problems with your kidneys?   Y   N

4. Do you get along with your mom?   Y   N

5. Are you currently in or have no problem attracting/maintaining romantic relationships?   Y   N

6. Do you hold grudges?   Y   N

7. Do you anger easily and stay angry?   Y   N

8. Do you love family and holiday get togethers?   Y   N

9. Do you have problems starting and/or finishing homework or new projects?   Y   N

10. Do you believe that synchronicity (coincidences) and luck are a part of your every day life?   Y   N

11. Do you have a problem getting and keeping money?   Y   N

12. Do you volunteer or are you generous with your time and money in other ways?   Y   N

13. Do you suffer from stomachaches or ulcers?   Y   N

14. Do you feel in control of your life and schedule?   Y   N

15. Do you feel stuck in a rut or a creature of habit?   Y   N

16. Do you get along with your dad?   Y   N

17. Do you suffer from headaches and migraines?   Y   N

18. Do you easily get help when you need it?   Y   N

19. Are you honest and true to yourself and live accordingly to your core values and morals?   Y   N

20. Do you take yourself and life too seriously?   Y   N

21. Do you laugh at yourself and life easily and often?   Y   N

22. Can you make decisions and stick to them once they are made?   Y   N

23. Do you take your studies and academic career seriously?   Y   N

24. Do you feel over-scheduled and rushed, like you don't have enough time?   Y   N

25. Are you passionate about something?   Y   N

26. Do you feel good when people recognize you or one of your achievements?   Y   N

27. Do you like yourself and the image you project?   Y   N

Now, compare your answers to the chart below. Example: Questions 1-3 correspond to the Career area, if you answered Y to questions 1 and 3, but N to question 2, you would only have 1 checkmark in the Career/Life Path area. This area is OK. However, if an area has 2 or 3 checks in it, this represents an area that may need some TLC.

Career/Life Path	Relationships	Family
1. N ___	4. N ___	7. Y ___
2. Y ___	5. N ___	8. N ___
3. Y ___	6. Y ___	9. Y ___
Wealth/Abundance	Health/Well-Being	Helpful People/Travel
10. N ___	13. Y ___	16. N ___
11. Y ___	14. N ___	17. Y ___
12. N ___	15. N ___	18. N ___
Creativity/Kids	Knowledge	Success/Fame/Luck
19. N ___	22. Y ___	25. N ___
20. Y ___	23. N ___	26. N ___
21. N ___	24. Y ___	27. N ___

OK, now that you've identified some areas that may need to be worked on or looked at, now what? Here is a brief description of the Bagua's nine life areas, why they are important and ways to "activate" them.

Career/Life Path

Let's start with the Career/Life Path area. If you don't know what you want to do with the rest of your life, don't stress out. A lot of people I went to college with (the first time!) were on the 6-year plan! I myself, changed majors three times, got a job right out of college that wasn't in my major AND ended up going back to school in my 30s when I decided on a career change. (It should be noted that I now have a career that encompasses what I enjoyed doing when I was a kid and in my teen years). My advice is to follow and pursue what you love doing. If you love to draw, go to art or design school. If you like math, check out business school for a career in finance or accounting. If you love to talk, look into a career in communications, journalism or teaching. If you have no talent or aptitude for something that you really enjoy (I love music but a career for me as a singer was NOT in the cards), look at taking these classes as an elective or a minor.

This area is to be activated (worked on) when you are applying for a new job, trying to get into the college of your choice or trying to decide on a major/career path. You can use the color BLACK and/or the WATER element here to bring about positive change in this area. Add an aquarium, water animal items (frog, turtle, fish …) and pictures, or a tabletop fountain to accessorize/activate this area.

A part-time job is a great way to increase your confidence, work experience, friend network, bank account and skill set. There are many things to look at in trying to find the perfect job that will fit into your schedule and personality. How many hours you can work with your school schedule, how you will get to and from your new job and your personality all need to be taken into consideration. If you're introverted look at data entry or working with plants and/or animals, if you're extroverted look at mentoring, coaching or retail as examples.

Now that you know what kind of job you want, finding the proper work environment is next. When interviewing, look at how the environment is organized, how clean the space is and the friendliness of the staff and supervisors. Here are some questions to ask yourself when applying for and interviewing for a job to see if it will be a good fit:

- Do the workers look happy to be there?
- Is the workplace neat and clean?
- Can you see yourself working and spending time in that environment?
- Is the space well lit?
- Do the customers look happy to be there?

If you get a "bad vibe" from the person interviewing you, from the clientele/customers or the employees, walk away and find someplace else to work.

Knowledge/Self-Empowerment

Next is the Knowledge/Self-Empowerment area. You are bombarded on a daily basis with more information than you could ever hope to process. The culprits include the TV, the Internet, school, music, advertising and friends. All of this "information" can turn into mental clutter and chaos if you aren't careful. You must learn to filter and distinguish what information is actually needed for your daily life and what is just mental clutter taking up valuable space in the recesses of your brain. Try sitting in silence for at least 5 minutes every day. Just sit and focus on your breathing while you let whatever thoughts enter your mind, as they will. Acknowledge these thoughts, and then let them go and return to focusing on your breathing. You will be amazed at how much calmer you feel and how much better able you will be at dealing with stress.

The Knowledge/Self-Empowerment area is where you want to do homework, study for a big test, meditate, and place any religious items you have. Your desk, books and computer should also be situated here. Use DARK BLUES and/or the EARTH element to help activate this area. Examples of the earth element are: stone figurines, a rock collection and/or crystals.

Here are some tools for you to use to get to know yourself better and feel comfortable in your own skin:

- Pay attention to your thoughts and self-talk. Are you your own best friend and personal cheerleader, or are you the first one to shoot down your ideas before they reach your lips? Would you treat or talk to one of your friends like you do to yourself? It is important to treat yourself with the same respect that you do all of your other friends.

- Keep a dream diary. Your dreams are your mind's way of letting you know what's going on in your heart and is a place for your creative self to express itself. A dream diary will help you remember and keep a record of all of those wonderful thoughts.

- Meditate. This will help quiet your mind and help you deal with stress and adversity. There are many meditation techniques that encourage you to calm your over-active mind and help you to attain the inner quiet and stillness that can connect you to your deepest reality-your true self.

- Keep a journal and write down your inner-most thoughts and feelings. You can learn many interesting things about yourself and your thought process. Every day sit down and just write for 15 minutes straight. Don't worry about punctuation, grammar or what you are writing, as journal writing is private. Through your journal, you can process your day, explore your dreams and desires, and organize your thoughts.

Still having problems getting in the study mood? Are you getting up every 5 minutes because you don't have a pen or book? Here are some tips to get your desk "study ready."

- Take inventory of your study supplies and make note of what you are missing (pens, scissors, paper, stapler …) and restock.

- Get an expandable file folder for important papers (report cards, references, pay stubs …) to keep them neat, organized and handy for when you need them (i.e. filling out a job or college application).

- Get a desk lamp if you don't have one, so you can see what you are doing.

- Avoid having your back to the door when seated at your desk, so you can see anyone entering your space.

Family

The Family area is one of the easiest to activate. This area should be focused on whenever you are experiencing family issues (i.e. you're not getting along with your younger brother!) or you want to maintain a harmonious family environment. Activate this area with natural GREENS (greens found in nature) and the WOOD element. Examples of items to use here are upward growing plants, wood furniture and/or accessories and happy family photos (especially in a green wood frame!)

This is a wonderful place for family photos. To increase the positive energy in this area, make a collage of your favorite family pictures. Pictures of your parents, siblings, cousins, grandparents, aunts, uncles and other special people whom you consider family should all be included. Be creative if you don't have photos of everyone (although this should encourage you to bring a camera to all family outings from now on). You can write down the names of "missing" family members and draw designs of your choice around the name to encourage positive feelings. Family crests, personal symbols or a picture of your home can also serve as the focal point of your collage.

Wealth/Abundance

The Wealth/Abundance area is the one I get asked about the most. You want to focus on this area when you'd like to get more money in your bank account, save for college or your first car, get a raise at work, keep the money you have coming in staying in your account or maybe you just want to live a more abundant, rich life (more friends, better quality items). This area is activated by the color(s) PURPLE/METALLICS and by the WATER element. Here you want to place a tabletop fountain, your coin collection/loose change jar, pictures of items you'd like to purchase, purple ribbons or an aquarium.

Do you want to increase your wealth and abundance even more?

- Increase abundance through symbols of generosity. Statues of open, giving hands symbolize charity. A large, open-mouthed bowl to collect your loose change for a donation to your favorite charity is a great reminder to help others, because as you give, so you shall receive.

- Strive for a simpler lifestyle. Think healthy, upward growing plants to attract wealth, growth and new opportunities.

- Focus on WHY you want more money, and then incorporate your answers into your design scheme. Example: if you'd like more money to shop at your favorite designer store, display the logo of the store (or a bag or box) in your wealth area. Think of the robin's egg blue color that symbolizes Tiffany's if a Tiffany's charm bracelet is your goal, or the green and gold of the Green Bay Packers if season tickets or stock is your dream. Be creative and think out of the box! Your piggy bank and/or your jewelry case can also be stored/displayed in this area to help activate money energy!

Success/Fame/Luck

The Success/Fame/Luck area is an area you want to energize when you'd like a promotion at work, get elected to a leadership position in student government (or any other organization you're involved in) or be noticed for your achievements. It should also be noted that this area is usually the focal point of most rooms. Here, use the color RED and the FIRE element. Candles, figurines of the sun, pictures of famous people and diplomas/certificates/trophies are all examples of items you can put in this area.

Relationships

The Relationship area is the second most asked about area of the Bagua due to the importance of family and friends in your life. This area should be worked on when you want to improve your relationship with your mom (your relationship with your dad is represented in another section), increase your circle of friends or to better existing relationships, improve your romantic visions/dreams and work relationships with co-workers. When thinking about all of the types of relationships there are in the world, you'd think there would be no common denominator or similarities, in how to deal with all of them, but there is. Here are some general tips to help you maintain and improve all of your relationships, current and future, and help keep them running smoothly.

- Say what you mean and mean what you say. Be as honest and straightforward as you can without being mean and cruel. You want to express yourself based on your beliefs and not on someone else's beliefs to get approval.

- Use "I" statements. These statements are declarations where all of the verbs are in the first person. "I feel …" not "You should …" is an example of taking ownership of your feelings and not putting the other person on the defensive.

- Listen. There's an old saying that we "have 2 ears and 1 mouth so we can listen twice as much as we talk." These are words all of us should live by.

- Protect yourself in all of your relationships. In other words, do not be a doormat for others. If you are in an unhealthy relationship (abusive, violent, negative, disrespectful), get out of it. If you find yourself trying to change to please another, pay close attention that the changes are positive and better yourself, not that you lose yourself and become someone you're not. If someone is constantly gossiping, being judgmental, cutting down others to make themselves feel better or belittling you and/or your dreams/accomplishments/goals-find another "friend." Negative people will bring you down and/or hold you back because of their fears, insecurities and jealousies. Surround yourself with people who will support and encourage you.

There are three colors used in this area: RED for legally binding relationships (marriage, legal business partnerships), PINK for single and looking for improvement and CORAL/PEACH for single and happy with single status. The EARTH element is the element used here. When looking to improve this area, use stones in the appropriate color (rose quartz is perfect), hearts, things in pairs, pictures of you with your friends or anything with a romantic connotation. While most of the above is directed at adults, you can still pay attention to and work on this area. Most teens aren't involved in "legally binding" relationships and just want to work on themselves and getting along with others. Guys and girls should pay attention to all shades of pink (go to a paint or home improvement store to see all of your choices) and use this color to activate this area. If pink still doesn't work for you, bring in personal items (hearts, pictures of you with your friends, items displayed in pairs to symbolize a couple or stones/crystals) that can accomplish the same purpose as color.

Creativity/Kids

The Creativity/Kids area should be activated when you are working on "giving birth" to a project. When you are having problems starting a particular project or if the word *procrastination* describes you, you want to address this area. This area is the perfect place to work on arts and crafts projects, journaling, writing or a tough homework assignment. Activate this area with the color(s) WHITE/METALLICS and the METAL element. Items to use here are: arts and crafts supplies, drawing easel, journal, metal accessories or any project you've created (i.e. photographs you've taken).

Helpful People/Travel

The Helpful People/Travel section is one of the harder areas to work on. Do you ever feel like the world is against you? Do you feel like you can't ever get a break or that you are always one step behind? You want to work on this area when you'd like some extra "help" in getting through a stressful time (like exams!), increase your support group or increase business in a fund-raising effort. The Helpful People/Travel area also corresponds to your relationship with your dad according to the Bagua board. (I told you dad wouldn't be forgotten!). This section, when aligned properly, will help bring about the right classes, parking spaces will open up, doors will be opened and people will be lined up to help you with whatever you need. This area also encompasses anyone and anything that supports you in your daily life AND the places you have traveled to or would like to go to (whew!).

Use the color GRAY and the METAL element. Here you can place photos of favorite teachers/mentors/bosses, angel figurines (or any religious items that lend support to you in times of crisis), photo albums, wind chimes, bells and photos of you and your dad on a happy occasion.

Not sure who the Helpful People are in your life? Here's a list of people that can be included in this area: teachers, counselors, friends/acquaintances, coaches, mentors, boss, siblings/relatives, animals/pets, police and religious leaders.

If you'd like to travel and expand your horizons, the TRAVEL area is where you'd like to focus. You could place a globe, atlas, photo albums from family trips or pictures or other symbols of places you'd like to travel to. This can include: postcards, figurines, ornaments, mobiles or a collage you've assembled.

Health/Well Being

Lastly, Health/Well-Being, which is the center section of the Bagua and, thusly, the center of any room or space, will be looked at. This is by far, the most important area of the Bagua because without your health, nothing else really matters. This area should be worked on continuously to help maintain good health and a healthy lifestyle. Choosing a lifestyle that supports the health of your body can improve not only the length of your life, but also the quality of it. A healthy body is more capable of clear thinking, positive emotions and energetic achievements.

If you want to avoid the trappings of bad habits, vices and negativity, look around your room at the posters and accessories you surround yourself with. Are there posters of musicians smoking? Do you have photos of airbrushed models promoting an unhealthy and unrealistic body image? What about ads promoting alcohol or smoking? Take them down and surround yourself with images promoting a healthy lifestyle and an environment that supports you and your endeavors. A tip to help you accomplish this, and to focus on what it means to be healthy, is to write down what it means to be healthy to you. Also, think about what habits you should acquire to be and stay healthy. Once you have this written down, think about what symbolizes these things, and then bring these items into your space.

It is imperative that this area be kept clutter-free at all times. You don't want any kind of blocks in this important section. This area is activated by EARTH TONES and the EARTH element. Again, keep this area free of clutter, dirt, furniture and other items. In some rooms, like a dining room, there is a table that is in the center of a room. In this case, keep the tabletop clear and clean with a plant/floral centerpiece and a bright ceiling light.

Here is a helpful chart to use once you have your room mapped out:

Area	Where located	Accessories	Colors to use
Career	Front middle	Water items, glass, mirrors, business cards	Black, dark blue
Knowledge	Front left	Books, computer	Blue, earth-tones
Family	Middle left	Family photos, plants, wood items	Green
Wealth/Abundance	Back left	Metal coins, plants, items that represent $ to you, water items	Purple, metallics
Success	Back center	Certificates, trophies, awards, pics of famous people	Red
Relationships	Back right	Hearts, candles, pics of friends, boyfriend/girlfriend, things arranged in pairs	Red, pinks, earth-tones
Creativity	Middle right	Art supplies, journal, computer, metal objects	White, metallics
Helpful People/ Travel	Front right	Globe, pics of places you'd like to travel to, chimes	Gray, metallics
Health	Center	Absolutely nothing	Earth-tones

Chapter 4
Your Environment and How it Affects You

The sights and sounds around us affect our well being, both consciously and subconsciously. We've all had noisy neighbors that have affected our sleep that in turn has affected our ability to perform at our best at school the next day. There's the neighbors in the next apartment who "think" they are gourmet cooks, much to the contrary smells coming from their apartment. Or the "artistic neighbor" who painted his house purple with polka dots "as a statement." (This happened in a neighborhood I lived in). Your environment is a major factor in how you interact with others as well as your mental and physical well-being. The goal of interior design is to create a space that is not only beautiful, but also takes into consideration all of the activities that are to occur in the space (sleeping, cooking, entertaining, meeting clients …). Feng shui takes design one-step further. Instead of working against your surroundings and trying to change them, you are working with and enhancing your environment. One of the ways you can "feng shui" your room, besides de-cluttering, is to try and get more "in tune" with your environment. I don't mean in a minimalist, no TV way (although if that's your idea of heaven, go for it). By utilizing all of your senses, you can create an environment that is balanced, more interesting and one that encourages you to interact more within your environment.

Let's address the five senses and how you can go about "engaging" them in your room. The five senses are: sight, sound, smell, touch and taste. The easiest sense to start with in design is sight. You see furniture. You see the view out of your bedroom window. You see your artwork. You can also see the clutter gathering under your bed. In talking about the sense of sight, if you don't have a positive association with an item, GET RID OF IT. Why do you want to look at something that makes you sad or angry? You want to surround yourself with items and be in an environment that gives you pleasure, that makes you happy and supports you. This topic will be discussed in-depth in the chapter dealing with clutter.

The easiest thing to "see" in your room is the color you choose to paint and/or accessorize your room with. But can color really make a difference? The color scheme you choose to decorate with says a lot about you and can even affect the way you sleep at night.

There are cool and warm colors. Cool colors are: blues, purples, blue/greens, and some whites. Warm colors are: reds, oranges, yellows, yellow/greens and some whites. Now, when speaking about color, remember that there hundreds of colors in a variety of tints (color with white added), shades (color with black added) and tones. Warm colors tend to excite and have been shown to raise our blood pressure. Use a warm color when you want to encourage activity. Think of the color schemes of fast food restaurants: red/orange/yellow: food eaten fast. Cool colors should be used when you want to rest or meditate. I always use cool colors in bedrooms to promote a better night's sleep. I'm not saying you can NEVER use a warm color in a bedroom or a cool color in a family room. I am saying you shouldn't use them as the primary color, but rather as an accent. Remember the meaning of the color and the activity of the room, and then match them.

Here are some of the meanings for primary and secondary colors:

RED—the most physical color, raises blood pressure, creates a sense of urgency, danger, excitement, vitality, ambition, anger. Too much red can cause irritation, impatience and anger. **PINK** is a gentler version of red and is soothing and calming, alleviates oversensitivity and surrounds you with a sense of love and protection. Research is being done on using this color in prisons to lessen violent tendencies in prisoners.

ORANGE—the color most linked with creativity, drama, and happiness-a wonderful anti-depressant. It is also the most uncomfortable color for most people. Orange is related to the digestive tract and increasing its function. For this reason, do not use orange as the primary color in a kitchen if weight is an issue, or if you are on a diet. **PEACH** is a gentler version and good for nervous exhaustion.

YELLOW—alertness, clear-headed, decisive, color of the sun. It is also one of the hardest colors for the brain to "break down." When using this color, make sure it's a clear and not dull yellow. Yellow is related physically with the nervous system-it excites. Use yellow sparingly if any of the inhabitants of the space exhibit any mental illnesses such as ADD, ADHD or hyperactivity. Never use yellow in a child's bedroom, rather, use earth tones. Yellow should be used primarily as an accent color. It is great for use in an office or any other room where mental functions/study are the primary activity.

GREEN—nature's color, the most balancing of the colors, related with the heart and regulating circulation, growth, new beginnings, comfort in times of stress. It is frequently the color choice in hospitals and is a perfect color in any room. Use yellow-greens sparingly, as it is hard on the eye. In general, any green found in nature can be used as a neutral.

BLUE—the most popular color, soothing, cooling, calming, lowers blood pressure, anti-inflammatory. Deep blue stimulates the pituitary gland, which helps to regulate deep sleep. It is the perfect color for bedrooms. Blue should not be used in a kitchen as it "grays out" the food and makes it unappetizing. However, if you are trying to lose weight, eat on a blue plate! Too much blue, especially dark blue, can be depressing.

TURQUOISE—refreshing, calming as it combines blue and green. Think of the waters off the Caribbean…. Ahhhhhhhhhhhh. It is invigorating, cooling and great when under mental strain. It is good for studios, studies, bedrooms, and bathrooms.

INDIGO/PURPLE/VIOLET—cooling, suppresses hunger, spiritual, peace, artistic endeavors. A great color for bedrooms, meditation rooms or any other room where quiet is emphasized.

WHITE—ultimate purity, peace, protection, cleansing, freedom. Too much can be cold and isolating. Use it in combination with any color. White is perfect in kitchens and bathrooms where cleanliness is key!

BLACK—protective, mysterious, associated with silence, passive. Too much black can be depressing, oppressive and indicate "hiding" from the world. Use as an accent with any color.

GRAY—independent, self-reliant, authoritative. Too much conotates fog, smoke, evasion and non-commitment (neither black nor white). Use as an accent color in an office or a teenager's room.

SILVER—emotional, sensitive, balancing, mentally cleansing. It is a great accent in a bedroom or bathroom.

GOLD—sunny, abundance, power, wisdom, understanding, energizing, inspiring. Gold is a perfect accent in an office, family room or kitchen.

BROWN/EARTH-TONES—color of Mother Earth, stable, is grounding, solid. Too much is boring and denotes an inability to move forward. Earth tones can be used as an accent with any color in any room.

****If you want to learn more about color and how it affects your life, check out the book "The Complete Book of Color" by Suzy Chiazzari. This is my color bible and I strongly recommend in to anyone who is interested in learning more about color.* ***

Does the sense of smell really apply to the overall design of a room? You bet! You know what smells good to you: fresh mowed grass, chocolate chip cookies baking in the oven, fresh flowers…. You also know what smells repulsive to you: a wet dog, burned food, garbage sitting out on a hot day … Your sense of smell is so strong and ingrained in your memory that a hint of certain smells can transport you back years in your memory bank to a place and time in your past-good or bad. Smell a rose and you're immediately transported back to being with your grandfather, as he tended his rose garden. You get the picture. The sense of smell is as important to design as your sense of sight. How can you enjoy that beautiful new bedroom and get a good night's sleep, if all you can smell is that fake lavender scented candle next to your bed?

Historically, perfume was first intended for use in "changing our surroundings" not for scenting our bodies. Ancient cultures, from the Greeks and Romans to the Chinese, relied on burning various plants to enhance their environment, and to influence and alter their bodies and minds in a therapeutic way. Now, with the home-fragrance industry topping $1.4 billion a year, we are being sold on "environmental fragrancing" as scents are being used everywhere from our home and car to restaurants and stores.

Since smell is tied to memory, surround yourself with scents that bring you back to times and places you enjoyed. I cannot emphasize enough that healthy, natural choices are imperative here. Many people are affected with environmental sensitivities, and the mere whiff of a synthetic perfume can send them grabbing their inhalers. So, if you or any family member are bothered by allergies, asthma or have any propensity to upper respiratory disorders, migraines and even fatigue-Go Natural! People also tend to respond to scent better if it is accompanied by a visual (i.e. pinecones displayed with a pine scent in a room,) hence potpourri's widespread use.

You can add scent to your space in a variety of ways:

- Add candles-look for soy, palm or beeswax with cotton wicks to avoid the smoking and sooting that can occur.
- Burn incense.
- Utilize fragrance wax or oil burners.
- Add potpourri (also plays into sight).
- Place light bulb rings on lights and use room diffusers.
- Use perfumed pillows and sachets.

***WARNING: Only burn candles or incense with your parent's permission, and never leave a burning candle unattended! ***

When choosing a scent, always take into account the activity of the room. You don't want to use lavender in a kitchen or peppermint in a bedroom. The scents of many plants have a psychological effect on us. All parts of plants and flowers are used and can be dried or harvested for their essential oils. When purchasing essential oils, or any of the above-mentioned items, look for natural ingredients and stay away from things labeled "fragrance," as these are man-made and use synthetic ingredients. These are usually petroleum based and can cause adverse reactions in people who have allergies, asthma, are prone to migraines/headaches or the elderly or very young.

Utilize these scents to enhance the environment of any room:

- Bergamot-clean, citrus/floral scent thought to be regenerating
- Grapefruit-clean, citrus scent thought to help balance appetite, lift the spirits and quell mood swings
- Green apple-fruity scent can reduce anxiety and claustrophobia
- Jasmine-a sweet floral scent believed to be an antidepressant, a tranquilizer
- Lavender-a floral/herbal scent that has been found to be relaxing, soothing, rejuvenating, deodorizing and anti-bacterial, believed to enhance the immune system and alleviate depression

- Lemon-a sunny, citrus scent found to be antiseptic and rejuvenating
- Orange-a tangy citrus scent thought to be uplifting and balancing
- Peppermint-a fresh scent found to be rejuvenating, antiseptic and cleaning
- Rose-a floral scent believed to be an antidepressant, a sedative and an antiseptic
- Rosemary-a spicy scent found to be antiseptic, regulating, astringent and mentally stimulating
- Sandalwood-a nutty, woody scent believed to be antiseptic, antidepressant
- Vanilla-a sweet orchid scent proven to be relaxing and reassuring

Let's examine the sense of touch next. We all know how a luxurious cashmere throw feels on a cold winter day as opposed to a cotton sheet. How about the difference between an Italian leather purse as opposed to one made of a nylon/polyester blend? I'm not trying to say that one texture is better than the other, but rather to highlight the difference and "feeling" you get when you touch and experience these things. Touch plays a big part in design and in creating the right "feel" (literally) of a space. You wouldn't put a comforter made of burlap in your bedroom, due to its rough and coarse texture, but you may have a couple of burlap pillows strewn across the floor. In design, texture is used to create VISUAL interest (there's sight again), create a more interactive experience and exciting space. Think of a child's playroom or schools that have walls with different textures to help kids learn and stimulate different areas of the brain.

The easiest way to introduce a variety of textures into your space is by adding accent pillows in a variety of materials to the bed or on the floor. A thick, luxurious throw on the back of a chair or even those bowls of balls, pinecones or marbles that proliferate every home décor store, all add interest to your space.

The next of the five senses is the sense of hearing. You can hide a bad view with curtains, a bad smell can be eradicated once the source is found, for touch you can add a pillow.... but a bad sound? You bet. The barking dog next door, the teenager down the block who insists his/her car stereo is stuck on 60, the neighbor who MUST mow his lawn at 6am ... we've all had experiences with bad sound. Sound proofing your room home with landscaping (talk to your parents to see if shrubs/bushes could be planted outside your window), heavy drapes and wall coverings (cork on the walls of your room can deaden the sound of their stereo-it also serves as a BIG bulletin board).

Another way to "deaden" outside sound is to place your heavy pieces of furniture against the walls where the sound is coming from. Try to place your bed on the opposite wall from where loud noises are coming from. A great example of this occurred with one of my students. Her bedroom is right off of the family room. The adjoining wall also happened to be where the TV and home theater system were placed. In this case, placing a bookcase filled with books and/or her desk would be the best bet. Also, an open, non-confrontational talk with other family members, in regards to the TV volume when she was in her room studying or sleeping, would also help.

The right choice in wall and window coverings can create a cocoon in your bedroom, and help to soundproof your space as well. If you have hardwood floors, a thick area rug and lots of pillows and books will help to absorb sound within the space. Music, wind chimes, pets (think of an aquarium and the hum of the filter, or your own barking dog), a TV or tabletop fountain all help to create atmosphere in your space. Sound is very personal. What is relaxing and comforting to one can be irritating to another. When adding or taking away sound from any space, check with other occupants and take their likes and dislikes into consideration when deciding to modify your room.

Here are some ways to control the volume in your space:

1. Make your room a haven of tranquility and your own personal sanctuary. To absorb sound, place rubber feet and/or foam pads under major electronic pieces (stereo, phone, and clock). Area rugs and thick curtains will also help to control and absorb sound. Think in terms of heavier fabrics (velvet, corduroy, duck cloth, leather, or micro fibers) as opposed to metal blinds or just sheers on your window.

2. Tune out the outside world. Concentrate on a pleasant view, daydream or put on headphones to "blot out" an unpleasant sound.

3. Give your brain a break. Play a white noise machine or play a blank tape or CD to tune out airplane, train or "neighborhood" noise. By doing this, you are turning your attention inward, and your mind can stop racing and worrying.

The last of the five senses is taste. Although not commonly thought of in terms of interior design, good foods and tasty treats not only make you feel better, but can contribute to an overall more pleasing environment. But DeAnna, you ask, how can I put food in my bedroom? It has been suggested a bowl of M&Ms in your room would be a positive addition, and can be incorporated easily. For the health-conscious, some fruit or trail mix on your nightstand or desk can also do the trick.

Let's examine how effectively using the five senses can improve your attitude, personal space and ultimately your life. When incorporating all of the five senses in your bedroom, start with sight. Pick out the proper color that is pleasant to all occupants of the space, as well as, fitting for the bedroom. Once the color scheme is selected, pick out the bedding and furniture. The furniture should fit the space and not be too big. Artwork should be calming in nature (no battle or violent scenes please!). Bedding is the perfect place to add texture (touch) in high thread count sheets, blanket, comforter and pillows. When adding sound, think soft music to set whatever mood you are trying to create. If you just want a good night's sleep, refer to the sound blocking ideas. Smell? Add a bowl of lavender or ylang ylang potpourri or candles to promote a restful sleep. At the very least, make sure bedding is fresh smelling. Taste can be accomplished with a pitcher of water at bedside to prevent the late night visit to the kitchen for something to drink. In conclusion, when utilizing the five senses in your room, and in all of your living spaces, you can create a balanced space, one that engages you as you and your friends or family interact within your surroundings.

In your quest to create a balanced space and lifestyle, and by keeping in mind the nine life areas of the Bagua board, adding the five elements to your space is an easy way to add excitement and really change the energy of a room. Plus, by prioritizing and focusing on which of the life areas you want to activate, the addition of the required element will help in achieving your goals. The five elements are water, fire, metal, earth and wood. You can add an element by adding an item made of the actual elemental material, or by the shape or color that represents its characteristics. Confusing, I know, but we'll try and make sense of it.

WOOD is an easy element to visualize. It includes furniture, plants, and figurines. Pictures of trees and forest landscapes are also representative of the wood element. Most of you can look around your room now and see at least one item that represents the wood element. Wood is also represented by the color green and by the shape of the rectangle.

EX; healthy green, upward growing plant

The element of **FIRE** is represented with candles or fireplaces. The sun and stars, pictures of famous people or people you admire, the stove and pyramids are also fire related objects. Fire is also represented by the color red, and by the shape of the triangle.

EX: a red candle

The element of **METAL** is usually seen in appliances, bath/kitchen fixtures or light fixtures. Metal can also be found in various accessories such as candleholders, sculptures, picture frames and coins. The color white and all metallics are associated with the Metal element and by the shape of a circle.

EX: a handful of coins

The **WATER** element is seen in pictures of the ocean, lakes, rivers, waterfall scenes), water-related animals (dolphins, frogs), table-top fountains, free-flowing fabrics (swagged curtains or draped throws) and mirrors. The color(s) blue and black, and free-flowing lines represent WATER.

EX: a tabletop fountain

The **EARTH** element is the hardest one for most people to visualize and implement in their home/room. Any item made from and found in the earth (clay, brick, stone, marble/granite and tile) can be used to represent this element. Do you have a terra cotta holder for a plant? You have Earth. Earth is represented by all earth tones and by the color yellow. The shape of a square represents Earth.

EX: a stone figurine of your favorite animal

Here is a table to help you remember the attributes of each of the elements and what you can add to activate or balance a life area:

Element	Attribute
WOOD	Blue and green, columns, stripes, spring, trees, plants, flowers
FIRE	Red, triangles, summer, sunlight, lamps, candles, people and animals
EARTH	Yellow and brown, squares, late summer, pottery, adobe, clay, brick, stone

METAL	White, metallics and gray, circles, ovals, autumn
WATER	Black, free and flowing organic forms, winter, glass, mirrors, windows

OK-let's examine how this can be achieved. The easiest room to start with is the bathroom. Most of you have at least 3-4 of the elements represented already in this space! Here goes. You have either tile on the floor, the walls and/or the shower-earth. Ceramic or vinyl floor tile is also usually square-earth. The bathroom is a water room with a tub, sink and toilet. The metal fixtures on the sink, tub and shower represent metal. Your vanity and cabinetry are typically made of wood. Plants are also commonly found in the bathroom, adding more wood. Your bathmats and towels are typically rectangle as well … wood again. Fire is the element that is usually missing. Adding candles and/or red/pink/burgundy to your color scheme can bring in fire. There, you now have all of the five elements represented in your bathroom! Not so hard, was it?

But DeAnna, I don't like/am afraid of color … how can I do this? Here's an example of how to create a balanced space without relying on color to make the difference. So, assuming a monochromatic color scheme, with a tan carpet and white walls, here goes. First, most of the furniture in your bedroom in made of wood. This would be your desk, dresser and/or nightstand. Your dresser and nightstand is also, typically, rectangular. More wood. Your bed is made of either metal or wood, or both, depending on the style. Plants will also bring in more of the wood element. All light fixtures in your room are made of metal (some may have wood accents) and electricity, which feeds your lights, represents fire. Candles will also add fire to your space. For water, a tabletop fountain is ideal. If you don't want that sound, pictures of water scenes, in wood or metal frames, will do the trick. The earth element can be brought in by a stone paperweight, crystals hanging in your window as sun catchers, terra cotta pots for plants or by square area rugs. Mission accomplished: a well-balanced room in a neutral color scheme.

Chapter 5
The Power Position and Auspicious Directions

The power position or focal point of a room is the spot where your eye immediately travels to upon entering a space. When I was designing retail spaces, the focal point/area was where we displayed our "featured" merchandise for the week, any seasonal items or anything that was featured in an ad or PR campaign. In a home setting, think of what says "you" or what sets the tone of the room. The WHY of creating a focal point is simple: a focal point gives the room a sense of purpose and helps determine the color scheme. The power position of the room is also the most psychologically secure position in the space. It is your starting point in any (re) design of the room. A focal point can be created using the room's major furniture piece (desk, bed, sofa …) a highlighted piece of artwork or an architectural feature. To find out where to place furniture or featured items, stand in the doorway of the space looking into the room and find the corner that is diagonal to the entryway.

Once that is determined, I start with how the room will be used as my starting point. In a bedroom, the bed is obviously going to be the focal point as it's the largest piece of furniture. You also spend a lot of money on bedding and pillows, making your bed a "work of art" and you want it to stand out. The bed, and other furniture focal points, are what "set the theme" of the room. It is the point of focus which will draw people in and add individuality to your room. An unfocused room can be as disconcerting as a blurry photograph: your eye doesn't know where to look.

A lot has been written about the "Death Position" of bed placement and the relationship to feng shui. The Death Position occurs when the bed is placed IN DIRECT LINE with the doorway resulting in the feet pointing out of the door when the occupant is sleeping. This position derived its name from the custom of carrying a dead body out of a room feet first. Therefore, when you sleep in this position, you are imitating a corpse (pleasant thought, hey?). But DeAnna, you say, there is no other place for me to put the bed, how do I counteract this? Well, there a few ways to alleviate the problem:

- You can use fabric to create a canopy over the bed. The fabric becomes a "wall" with the bed then sitting in a niche. This also creates a cocoon of sorts and gives the feeling of security.
- Place a faceted crystal between the bed and door.
- Place a folding screen at the foot of the bed (see first tip).

Your bed should have a headboard for support and give you a feeling of security when you sleep. The bed should also be raised off of the floor for chi/energy to flow around you as you sleep. There should also be no clutter or anything else stored under your bed as sub-consciously you would be sleeping over your clutter and any unresolved issues represented by these items. That being said, you also shouldn't have a bed that has drawers under it, however, if this is the bed that you have, make sure that the drawers are kept neat and organized. Again, you don't want to be sleeping on unresolved issues and chaos!

Once your bed is perfectly positioned, lie down. What do you see? Hopefully you see something pleasant-a picture of you and your best friend, some candles or the garden outside of your window. If you see the bathroom, your neighbor's dead tree or nothing … change the view. The view you see first thing in the morning or right before you close your eyes for the night sets the tone subconsciously for the day or your dreams. Make it positive.

Now that you know what the power position is, and how to find and utilize it in your room, let's kick it up a notch and figure out your auspicious directions and pa-kua number. The pa-kau number is your lucky number. This number is also used to determine if you are a West or East group person (the primary grouping of directions used to determine what areas are best for you to face). Once you calculate your auspicious (good/positive) directions you will know which way to face when giving a presentation in class, which direction is most "healthful" for you to sleep in and to use for space planning the rest of your furniture. Let's calculate your pa-kau numbers.

For Guys:

Subtract your year of birth from 100 and divide by 9. The remainder is your number. If there is no remainder, your number is 9.

EX: for a guy born in 1990
100-90=10. 10 is divided by 9=1 with a remainder of 1

EX: for a man born in 1955
100-55=45. 45 divided by 9=5 with NO remainder; therefore the number used is 9

For Girls:

Subtract 4 from your year of birth and divide by 9. The remainder is your number. If there is no remainder you must take the number 9.

EX: for a girl born in 1990
90-4=86 divided by 9=9 with a remainder of 5

EX: for a woman born in 1949
49-4=45 divided by 9=5 with NO remainder. Therefore the number used is 9.

Best and Worst Directions:

The number located in the center is the pa-kua number. Also note that if you get the #5 as your pa-Kua number, there is a different set of numbers for guys and girls. Make sure you are looking at the correct diagram!

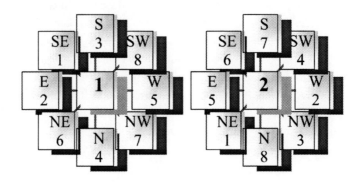

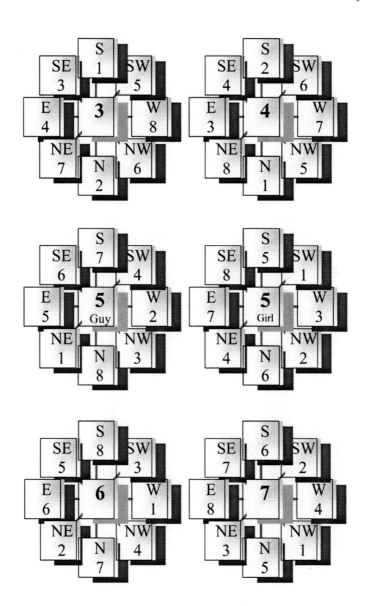

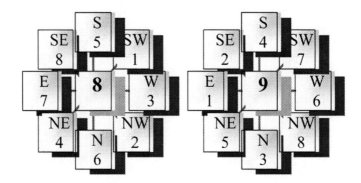

All right, so what do all of these numbers mean? Following is the order of the best and worst directions and what they represent.

1. Abundance and happiness, if all other aspects of your life are in order (clutter-free and running smooth). Try and have your headboard in this direction if possible.

2. Health

3. Family harmony

4. The self-perfect place for a desk.

5. Mishaps-things will not go as planned here

6. Arguments at home, school and work

7. Legal and health problems

8. Disaster-avoid this direction at all costs

When using these directions, you should always try and face one of the first four and avoid the last four whenever possible. If you are able to choose your seat in class, are able to choose where you stand in giving an oral presentation or have flexibility in placing your bed or where you sit at the dinner table, utilize one of your four best directions and see what positive changes occur!

Chapter 6
Clutter—Are you Calm and
Collected, or Scattered and
Frazzled?

After a long hard day of classes, tests, piano lessons and an extended gossip session with your best friend, all you want is a little peace and quiet. Your bedroom is the best place for this, as it is the one place in your house that is yours. It is your shelter, personal sanctuary and safe haven from the outside world. It's also a reflection of you and your life as you currently live it. So, what does your room say about you? Neat and organized? Calm and collected? Do you have scattered piles of unfinished projects and homework all over your desk? This chapter is for you!

*** *By saying "sayonara" to unloved, un-needed items you will give chi free reign to flow.* ***

Clutter is defined as anything you don't use, need, want or love. Clutter is related to stagnant energy in the house and in your life. If you don't use something, or if you don't need or even particularly want something and it doesn't make you happy or there is no positive association with an item…. why do you keep it? We all keep items because we USED to like them or we paid a lot of money for them. There is a real fear associated with getting rid of an item-ANY ITEM. We are afraid that we won't be able to replace it, or that we are letting go of our past and associated memories or the all too familiar guilt. Let's address the fear of replacing the item. First, why are you worried about replacing an item that you aren't using, want or like? Secondly, if you do need the item, chances are there is a new, improved and cheaper model available. Get rid of the old!

The second fear is one of the hardest to deal with, as there are frequently so many memories invested in some of our collectibles or "family heirlooms," it's the fear of forgetting the person or event that surrounds an item. That being said, there are some items that have extraordinary meaning-a pressed flower from a prom corsage, your first stuffed animal, a card from your best friend … all things that can be kept and displayed for you to enjoy. However, EVERY card you ever received or EVERY stuffed animal ever bought does not qualify. Be selective. This fear really comes into play when dealing with the loss of a loved one, whether a friend, relative or schoolmate. You fear that by getting rid of the departed one's picture, a gift you received from them or any item that reminds you of them, you are in essence "getting rid" of that person from your memory, thought and heart. This is not true—*Memories are in our hearts not our things!*

Lastly, we feel guilty if we get rid of something. The item can be a piece of clothing, a knick-knack or an expensive gift. For example, I have a friend who was given a cashmere sweater by her then boyfriend. They broke up. She kept the sweater and continues to wear it. She would receive compliments on the sweater, but every time she wore the sweater or had to answer where she got the sweater, it made her think of her EX, bringing up all of the memories associated with him and their now ended relationship. She stopped wearing the sweater because of all the bad memories associated with wearing it, but she wouldn't donate it, as "it was expensive." So to sum up, she kept an item that she used to like and whenever she wore or saw it, it brought up very intense negative emotions, but she wouldn't get rid of it because it was an expensive item. If something you have/ own doesn't make you happy, or at the very least, doesn't make you cry (!) why do you keep it? If you don't love it-get rid of it. By hanging on to old things/ items, you are really hanging on to emotional baggage.

***Ancient feng shui secret: Live with what you LOVE! ***

OK, so now you know what to look for or how you should feel when you start to go through and organize your belongings and collections, but HOW do you start? A quick three-step process follows:

1.   Give yourself permission to let go of things.

2.   Donate/sell/toss what you don't need, love or use.

3.   Organize what's left.

The first one is the hardest and probably what stops people from even getting started in the process. It is OK to let things go and move forward. If your home and life are "cluttered," how can you experience growth and allow new things to enter your life. This can be in the form of new items, experiences or relationships.

In feng shui terms, each area of your room/house corresponds to a different life area. Is there an area that you're having problems with? Is there an area where you'd like to see some sort of change to occur? Refer to the Bagua chart to see which life area is cluttered and how it applies to your life currently. Is your bank account always near zero? Do you have trouble concentrating at school or when doing homework? Do you start projects but never seem to finish them? Clear up the clutter and see what happens!

Here are some tips to help you lead a clutter-free life:

1. Start small-a drawer, a closet, your purse ... then the task isn't so daunting.

2. Evaluate your items one at a time-ask yourself if you really love, need, want or use the item. If the answer is NO to any of the above, get rid of it.

3. Sit down and make a list of what you really need and what you want. You'll be surprised at what you already have and what you have that you thought you needed. Do you really need more than one hair dryer? (When I did this I actually had 3 hair dryers-just in case one broke and one for travel!)

4. Give yourself a homework assignment. Clean one drawer a day/week ... this will give you a sense of accomplishment and will help to break down the overall task.

5. Get outside advice. Sometimes it's hard to be objective regarding certain items (i.e. clothes, collections ...). It's OK to bring in a 3rd party, whether it's a friend or family member. Remember to not take what they say personally, and that they are there to help you. You may get to return the favor!

6. Use existing storage. If you have too much stuff, it's easy to run out to the store and buy more storage containers. Instead of going out and spending more money on something you don't need, utilize the storage and space that you currently have. You will be surprised at all of the extra space you now have and nothing to put there!

7. Stop before you buy anything else. ALWAYS ask yourself "why" you want to purchase the item. We tend to buy on want as opposed to need. If you decide that you do need the item, let go of one item you currently have to make room for the new item. The famous artist Georgia O'Keefe would only bring home a new item after getting rid of an old item in her home.

OK, you're all set to start purging your clutter. You need to set up 3 piles: keep, sell/donate, and toss. BE BRUTAL! If you are starting with a drawer, empty out the drawer. If you are starting with a closet, empty out the closet. Only put back what you LOVE, USE and WORKS. Period. These are your KEEP items.

Items to SELL/DONATE are things that you don't respond positively to in the above questions. Have a rummage sale; sell on eBay; put an ad in the paper. These are all effective ways to sell unwanted items. Make sure to talk it over with your family first. This can be a great way to get other family members motivated to get rid of their junk. You can also suggest doing something "family oriented" with all of the money you get from selling your stuff: a nice dinner, some new electronic equipment for the family room, new DVD/CDs or a baseball game. Have fun with this and make it an activity you can all take part in and you can all see the rewards of. When deciding on what can be sold, make sure the item is still in usable condition, that all pieces are there and work like they are supposed to and that the item is clean. Price accordingly. You must be prepared to toss or donate any items that don't sell.

If you decide that you just want the "stuff" out of your space, donating the item is your best bet. Some charitable organizations will even pick up your items for you! There are many organizations to choose from: Salvation Army, Purple Heart, and Goodwill. These are some of the larger organizations; however, there are many other organizations that will take donations. Donate those books, toys, puzzles and games to a Ronald McDonald house, library, children's hospital or shelter for the homeless of abused and battered families. Check your Yellow Pages to see what's in your area and their policies. Again, check with your parents before doing this. They may have some items to go as well!

Toss those things that are broken and can't be fixed, are ripped and/or torn or just junk that you've accumulated. Get a dumpster if you have to. After my father died, my Mom started what began as just clearing out some of my father's things into a one-year project that cleaned out the house from top to bottom. Literally, two dumpsters were filled, as my brother and I helped my Mom purge thirty years of accumulated stuff.

Now, let's talk about clothes clutter. We all have it. We have school clothes, sloppy clothes, and dress-up clothes.... Ahhhhhh. The problem is also compounded depending on what part of the country you live in. If you live in a northern climate, your wardrobe must include cold, wet and warm weather variations of the above-mentioned clothes. Your wardrobe should reflect the person you are now or would like to be, not who you were. Think about dressing like your older sibling or co-worker/boss whom you admire! If your wardrobe looks like a throwback to your pre-teen days or only represents one facet of your life (i.e. only dresses, but no jeans, or only athletic shoes and sweats, but no dress clothes), you need to carefully evaluate your clothes and see what they may say about your current life situation. Do you like what your wardrobe says about you?

From a feng shui stand point, if your wardrobe is unbalanced-representing only 1 or 2 life areas-look at what's missing. Is it an area you want to improve upon or work on? A friend was evaluating her wardrobe and getting ready to purge items when she realized that she had no "date" clothes. This came as quite a shock. Nothing was found that could even come close to being described as feminine or romantic. What is interesting about this is that this person was working on her Relationship area and really was trying to make an effort to improve that part of her life. Needless to say, that next weekend she grabbed one of her most objective friends and went to the mall. Her confidence and focused attention on this area has improved, which has brought about more opportunities in this life area. Again, look at your wardrobe and see what it is reflecting about your life. Do you like it? If not, change it.

It can't be stated enough that if you don't have positive feelings and/or use your "stuff," you shouldn't have it. It's OK to give yourself permission to let things go and then DO IT. Once you start on your "purge," you will be amazed at how much stuff you are ready to part with. If you are like my Mom, you will even start looking for more things to get rid of once you are finished. You may even get your parents and siblings motivated! I still go through my closets and am amazed at some of the clothes that have escaped previous purges. I've started looking at the items I'm getting rid of and considering what I could have done with that money instead (a new CD, a month's worth of Starbucks ... you get the idea).

Remember:

- If you don't love it, use it or need it-Get RID of it!

- If you've outgrown items (toys, clothes …)-Get RID of them!

- If an item is broken, and you haven't fixed it, replaced it, or missed it—Get RID of it!

- If your clothes, collections, books … don't say who you are right now or where you want to be-Get RID of them!

- Give yourself permission to let go of items that you are hanging onto due to guilt or fear.

- Love what you have. You should enjoy your "stuff" not be stressed out by it.

- Use your stuff. Don't save things for "that special occasion." Everyday is special and should be treated as such. Make up a holiday or just celebrate the fact that you remembered your locker combination! Celebrate yourself and your life.

A sense of clarity and a sense of control over your space will wash over you as you can now actually see your space and you living in it! You should own your stuff-it doesn't (or shouldn't) own you!

In evaluating whether to keep or get rid of your artwork and collections, ask yourself what the "theme" is. Meaning, do you have a collection of hunting items (includes arrowheads, bow and arrow sets, BB guns, water guns, etc.) or cat figurines. One has violent connotations, while the other has a more passive connotation. We can take it one step further to see what kind of cats is being displayed: domestic cats or tigers. See the difference? It should be noted that I have designed rooms with a "southwest theme" where arrowheads and Indian bow and arrows played a prominent role. I kept these displays away from the bed (I placed dream catchers there) and made sure none of the items were pointing at the bed from where they were hanging. This is especially important if you have problems sleeping at night, as subconsciously, you will "feel" these weapons pointing at you.

Where the items are being displayed is also important. In feng shui, you must also look at what a room's purpose is. The bedroom reflects rest. The family room is for social/entertaining/family gatherings. Your artwork, collections and colors should enhance the purpose of the room, and be inspiring and meaningful. Otherwise, the artwork adds nothing to the space and the room can look unbalanced, uninviting and blah. Remove any images that are hung up only to cover up a bare wall. Each picture, poster and item used to accessorize your room should serve a purpose and add something positive to the space, not just "take up space," literally.

Here are some tips:

- Decorate your bedroom door with things that represent who you are. A bulletin board hung on the door is ideal as you can easily change photos, ticket stubs and articles as the mood strikes or as your taste changes.

- Use welcoming symbols such as bells. (This can also serve as warning if an irritating younger sibling tries to sneak into your room!).

- Make sure your windows have some sort of covering on them. This will help you sleep better at night, and can help reduce outside noise as well (use heavy drapery in this case).

- Mirrors should be avoided in the bedroom if possible, especially if you have problems sleeping at night as mirrors increase the energy moving around in the room. Hang mirrors on the inside of your closet door if possible. If this isn't an option, cover them with fabric at night. Also, look at what your mirror is reflecting … it better not be clutter! Hang your mirror so that you can see as much of you as possible and that the mirror reflects something positive and attractive, not a blank wall.

- Wind chimes can be used inside as well as outside. Hang a chime in your window so it makes a sound as the breeze blows in or place it above your desk for you to ring as you sit down to study. It will help clear out the cobwebs!

- Bamboo can be used to enhance positive energy in your space. It represents growth in all facets of your life. Lucky Bamboo plants can be found at most home improvement stores and garden centers.

- Music is one of the best feng shui cures in creating positive energy in your space. So surround yourself with music that makes your heart sing. Use music to motivate, cheer you up after a bad day at school, or to help you get to sleep.

Chapter 7
Feng Shui in School, Social and Family Situations

Having problems in school? Final exams got you down? You can use feng shui principles to help in your academic career. First, look at the Knowledge area of your bedroom. Is your desk and computer here? Is it clutter free or a mass of books, notebooks and paper? If this is the case, re-visit the clutter chapter. If not, here are some tips to help you:

- At home, hang a crystal over your desk to increase the chi.

- Place a piece of amethyst on your desk to increase your concentration when you study. You can even use a larger piece as a paperweight!

- If organization is an issue, color-code each class. Match up notebooks and folders to each subject-maybe match them to the book's cover to help.

- On your computer, delete old emails, files and folders that you are done with. It will lessen the "clutter" you have to wade through to get to the file that you need.

- If your desk is by a window, make sure that there are curtains to close when you study, so you aren't compelled to go outside and play when you need to concentrate.

- When choosing your seat in class, avoid sitting by the window as well. This will cut down on daydreaming and force you to pay attention to what the teacher is saying. Instead, try and sit front and center.

- Stay away from the back row in a classroom, as there are too many distractions and it's too easy to "hide."

- Sit under a light. Dim lighting can make you drowsy and is bad for your eyes as it causes eyestrain.

- Use color to keep you in the scholarly mood: choose light green notebooks for subjects that stress you out, decorate your locker with yellow to keep you upbeat throughout the long school day, dress in navy blue to look smart (and for when you have to give oral presentations) and use rainbow stickers on school supplies or in your locker to keep in harmony with your surroundings.

Make sure the Knowledge area of your bedroom is clutter-free (!) and organized. You want to be able to access books, notebooks, folders/files, pen and computer when you need them and make the most of the time when you are in "that study mode." The color blue should be used here as well. If blue isn't in your room's color scheme, bring in blue with fresh flowers, picture frames or a blue area rug under your desk and chair.

OK-you've got school and studying aced, but how do you increase your circle of friends and get along better with your siblings and parents? You can apply your newfound knowledge of the Bagua board, and how to activate the nine life areas, to your wardrobe (ex: where red to a party to get noticed by more people), to where you sit in the library (ex: sit in the Knowledge area to maximize study time) and by reducing clutter in the Family area or your bedroom to help improve a positive "energy flow" in your relationship with your bossy, older sister.

Let's address your social life, friends and romantic, by starting in the Relationship area of your bedroom. Make sure it's clutter-free. If not, go back and review the clutter chapter. Here is where you want to display all the photos of you and your friends having fun. Place a bulletin board here where you can add photos, invitations, calendar and ticket stubs.

Your Relationship area is where you should place a photo of you and your boyfriend/girlfriend. If you don't have a boyfriend/girlfriend, but would like to date more (with parent's approval), try placing items in pairs. Items displayed singularly (one) represents being solo, and things displayed in threes mean a third person always coming between you and your boyfriend/girlfriend/best friend. Pink is the color of choice here. I know some of you will cringe at the thought of PINK (ugh), however, this is the color used to activate this area and the color of self-love. Self-love means loving and liking yourself, which you need to do before anyone else will feel that way about you. A simple and great way to activate this area is to find a rose quartz heart as this brings in the color pink and the earth element. Hearts also symbolize love! For the guys who want nothing to do with pink hearts, try a piece of pink cloth or a pink ribbon and hide it under a book. A feng shui "cure" unseen works just as well as a "cure" that is seen. It's the intention and thought towards a goal that is really at work here.

When working on the Relationship area, you can't just hope that by placing a heart in this area all will be perfect with your friends or that you will meet/date/marry the person of your dreams. You need to get out there and try to make things happen. Here are some tips on how not to be a wallflower:

- Relax.... take a deep breath as a calm you creates a confident approachable you.

- Remember the Bagua board! Look at where the Relationship or Success areas are at a party, the lunchroom, study hall ... wherever kids congregate and observe what happens. Then get yourself over there and take part.

- Stand straight. Think clean and graceful lines when standing or sitting, as awkward angles look awkward and uncomfortable and unapproachable.

- Most importantly, be yourself. You have a lot to offer, don't settle for less or lower your expectations.

- Wear shimmery pink lip-gloss for your next date to appear charming to the cute guy in your English class. For the guys, wear a red sweater to add some excitement and to get noticed by that cute girl in your homeroom.

You also need to look at how approachable you are by taking a hard look at your body language. Body language is the way you stand, the way you walk and how you position your body when in class, at your locker, talking with your friends or sitting by yourself in the lunchroom. Here are some Do's and Don'ts to keep in mind and observe in yourself, to see how "approachable" you are.

DOs

The Move	The Meaning
Open arms, lean forward	Engaged, involved
Smile, arms behind back	Attentive
Nod, tilt head	Attentive, interested

Don'ts

The Move	The Meaning
Tap foot, stare into space	Bored
Clenched hands	Defensive, annoyed
Looking around	Distracted, uninterested

Now that you've got some new friends, or have re-connected with your current group, here are some party ideas with a "feng shui twist."

The first one is for a Yin party. Yin brings about the quiet, relaxing, cooling and feminine principles of the Yin/Yang symbol. You want to have a Yin party (or just bring some Yin into your life) when you want a relaxing, rejuvenating party where you can talk and connect with your friends. This can be for a good "chit-chat" with your girlfriends or watching a sporting event with your guy friends. Decorate in blues, grays and purples with bamboo stalks and bowls of oranges (great for a late night snack!) for abundance and happiness. Serve foods that are light and cooling:

- Cucumber and Tomato Sandwiches-Cucumber, tomato and lettuce make this simple sandwich. Remember to take off the crusts and cut into little triangles to make special.

- Fruit Salad w/Ice Cream and Honey-Cut up apples, oranges, strawberries or any other fruit you'd like. Serve with a big scoop of vanilla ice cream and drizzle with honey. Yum!

- Citrus Splash-Fill glasses with ice cubes and seltzer, then squeeze in fresh orange and lemon juice.

- Warm Peppermint Tea w/Honey—On those cold fall/winter nights, put a kettle on and make a pot of peppermint tea. Stir in a spoonful of honey. Mmmmmmmm....

- Salsa and other Dips w/chips-A tomato salsa with tortilla chips or veggies with dip are a good cooling treat for a night of watching TV or movies. You also don't have to be a chef to put this together for your friends.

The second is a Yang party. Yang means fun, action, heat and lots of socializing. A Yang party is for a huge group of people to dance, talk and mingle to the wee hours. Decorations for this party should include: reds, lanterns, bright lights and lots of dance music. Serve foods that are rich, dark, warm and gooey:

- Cheese Roll-Ups-Roll pieces of chicken or ham (can use vegan alternatives) with lettuce and cheese. Stick a toothpick through the center of each roll to keep together.

- Peanut Butter and Chocolate Graham Cracker Sandwiches-Break a chocolate bar into large pieces. Spread peanut butter onto each piece and sandwich it between two graham crackers.

- Chocolate Shake-Break up a couple of chocolate bars and stick them in a blender with one cup of ice cream and one cup of milk. Blend on high until smooth and creamy.

- Banana Boats-Slice a banana down the middle and alternate chocolate chips and mini-marshmallows in the banana. Wrap in aluminum foil and bake for 5 minutes at 300 degrees (until the chocolate is melted). Really gooey and good!!!!

Some other feng shui food for your soul:

- Fortune cookies-corny, yes, but who doesn't rip open that cookie waiting to see what the fortune cookie gods say waits in store for us?

- Mangos-represents abundance

- Oranges-represent abundance and happiness

- Noodles and peanuts-ensure a long life

- Steamed dumplings-for good fortune

All right, you have been working on your grades and your social life is going gangbusters, but what about your irritating little brother or your parents who are just embarrassing? You want to first look at the Family area of your room and make sure it's clutter-free. If not, refer back to the clutter chapter. This area is where you want to display family photos. When deciding on what photos to use, look for pictures that show you happy with all of your family members. Make sure all of your family members are pictured and that you are in the photos as well. This will give the energy of you all literally being one big happy family. To really "feng shui" your family, find the Family area in your house and apply the same tips.

Look at the bathroom in your home as well, especially if you have to share a bathroom with your siblings. Clutter in the bathroom is a given in most homes, but it shouldn't be. Involve your parents and siblings in on de-cluttering this space. Get rid of all old, expired medications and make-up (6 months is the norm) as they are past their usefulness and effectiveness. Do a thorough cleaning of the sinks, tub and toilet (natural cleaners please!). **It is important that when working on spaces shared with other family members, that you get your parents permission. Include them in the process and use this as on opportunity to find common ground and create some new memories.** Here are more bathroom tips:

- Keep all drains covered (no exposed pipes), seats down and door shut. You don't want all the good energy to "go down the drain!"

- Hang a crystal between the door and toilet if you see the toilet immediately upon entering the space. A small plant on the tank of the toilet will also keep energy moving up.

- Make sure the mirror is large enough and hung to reflect your head, and all who use this room.

- Use décor in here that will bring your eye up. Wallpaper border is perfect here! Funky lights and upward growing plants will also keep your eye, and energy moving up.

- Turquoise candles will help you feel pampered and relaxed.

Chapter 8
Keeping Your Room GREEN and Healthy

EMFs, VOCs, oh my! No, this isn't some foreign language, but rather acronyms for some potentially serious items that could affect your health. EMFs, or electro-magnetic field, are emitted by every piece of electronic equipment (TV, computer, computer, clock radio …) that is in your room and home. As long as an electric cord is plugged in, an electric field is active. Magnetic fields are active once a device is turned on. Studies have shown that EMFs disrupt your central nervous system and can affect your sleep patterns. In some cases/studies, it has been shown to adversely affect your health with higher rates of cancer, migraines and fatigue. Phones and clocks, which are considered necessities in a bedroom, should be kept an average of 3 feet away from the headboard of the bed. Keeping the clock further away will also prevent you from abusing your snooze button! I've had many people disagree with me about having a TV and/or computer in the bedroom stating they "need to have the TV on to fall asleep" or "there's no other place for the computer." I suggest a closed entertainment center for the TV and other electronics, including CDs, DVDs and video gaming equipment. This way, the doors can be closed when items are not in use. There are also closed desk units that can be used to "hide work" when you are transitioning the bedroom for sleeping and not studying.

Live, healthy plants will also help to cut down on the ill affects of your can't-live-without technology. Try philodendrons, peace lilies and palm trees for the best results.

VOCs are volatile organic compounds that are the chemicals and toxins that are emitted into the air by the off gassing of paint, newly installed carpet, PVC/plas-tics and/or stains and adhesives used in construction and remodeling projects. These VOCs can cause and/or irritate any upper respiratory illnesses, headaches, allergies and dizziness. That new paint or new car scent you smell upon walking into the room or sitting in the car is actually the chemicals being emitted into the air that you are breathing in. This isn't good. If you are looking at new carpeting or paint in your room, look for no VOC paint (available from all major paint manufacturers), air out the new carpet BEFORE it's installed (most installers will do this if asked upon purchase) and look for the green or healthy alternatives in furniture and textiles. Ask if you don't see anything listed on a label or want some clarification on something listed.

If you suffer from allergies and/or asthma, paying attention to VOCs and dust in your room is a must to discourage attacks or to keep them to a minimum at the very least. Here are some tips:

- If you have wall-to-wall carpeting in your room vacuum weekly-daily if you have pets that sleep with you, to get rid of the dust mites and dirt that collect in the fibers.

- Use natural cleaners to clean mirrors, windows and furniture. Natural cleaners are available at most groceries and on the Internet. Household cleaners are in the top five of indoor air pollutants due to the chemicals used in the manufacturing process. These chemicals are emitted into the air, and like VOCs, you breathe them in, thusly, affecting your lungs and breathing. Read the labels-if you can't pronounce an ingredient, look for an alternative.

- If you have a trashcan in your room, don't let garbage build up to the point of over-flowing. In feng shui terms, trash is reflective of the garbage you carry around in your daily life. So, don't let the garbage build up in your room or elsewhere! You'll feel so much happier.

Did you know that live plants are a natural detoxifier? The optimum formula is one plant for every 100 sq feet. If you have a 10x10 bedroom (standard) this means you need 1 plant. Plants are also good in terms of feng shui as they bring energy and life into a space (if well-tended!). When you are using plants to acti-vate an area (primarily in the Family, Career, Success and Wealth areas), make sure it is upward growing-no vines or ivies-as this will bring energy down. Sug-gested plants are: jade, bamboo, spider plants, philodendrons (keep pets away as they are poisonous to cats and dogs), peace lily, Boston Fern, corn plants and fichus. Each of these plants is relatively easy to care for and is great for removing chemical vapors (VOCs) from the air. Use your instincts when choosing a plant for your space-if you don't like it or if the plant looks out of place, don't use it.

Stay away from plants that are droopy or sad looking, you want to bring in life and energy. Always remember to trim dead leaves and dust as needed.

We spend 1/3 of our lives sleeping. Make sure it's quality sleep with as high a quality mattress that you can afford. This goes for bed linens as well. Go for a high a thread count in the sheets for that soft, luxurious feel that makes you want to get into bed! Great, inexpensive linens can be found in a variety of fabrics. Some of the larger chains (Linens and Things and Bed, Bath & Beyond) even carry bedding made of bamboo fibers! Fibers for your bedding and towels include: organic, unbleached cotton, jute, wool, silk and bamboo. All of these items are available in a variety of colors and patterns.

If allergies and environmental sensitivities are an issue, hypoallergenic alternatives are available as well. Pillows, mattress pads, bedding and comforters are all made now from natural fibers and dyes that won't aggravate an illness. Pillow and mattress casings are also available to prevent dust mites and other things that can trigger an attack.

The right pillow should also be purchased to promote a healthy night's sleep. Pillows are made for people who sleep on their sides, back and stomach. They are also made in a variety of materials from down, poly-fills and rubbers that will mold to your head/neck for better support. Visit a bedding store and look at all of your options.

***Remember, a healthy night's sleep will promote a better next day! You will feel refreshed and more alert to meet all of the day's challenges, both mentally and physically! ***

Chapter 9
Conclusion

Well, your journey is finished (at least as far as this book is concerned), and I hope that you have learned some useful skills that you can apply to help you achieve the life of your dreams. You have learned some basic feng shui principles: how color can affect you (mentally and physically), the effects of clutter (mentally and physically) and how having an understanding of the Bagua board and how to activate the nine life areas, can help you take control of your life and not just be a by-stander.

In conclusion, I'd like to offer a few tips for your Very Important Space to make room for new growth and opportunities:

- De-clutter: There should be nothing under the bed as this, in feng shui terms, causes you to be sleeping on unresolved issues. From a health standpoint, it doesn't allow for proper air circulation around you. This goes for your desk, purse, car, wallet and school locker! If you don't love it, use it or need it-get rid of it!

- Excessive electronic gadgets in the bedroom, or any room, are troubling from a health aspect due to the high levels of EMFs being emitted into the space. If you have problems sleeping at night or suffer from headaches and fatigue, look at the amount of electronic equipment that you have in your room and remove them.

- Paint your room a cool color to help lower heart rate and blood pressure, and to promote a good night's sleep. Remember, you sleep better in a "cool" room, so think of a color scheme in blues, purples and greens.

- Utilize your power position to feel psychologically secure in the space.

- Have FUN. This is a process and you will make mistakes. You will also need to re-evaluate your room every few months, as your goals/priorities in certain life areas will change, as you get older. What works for you at 14 will be much different as you turn 18 and are getting ready for college.

- Remember that change is a good thing, and is merely an opportunity to grow and learn something new. It can be as small as changing the type of sheets on your bed (cotton has a much different feel than polyester) to finding your new locker at a new school. Meet each new challenge with confidence and make the most of your life.

- Lastly, stay true to yourself and your beliefs. Be honest in your dealings with others (from your obnoxious younger brother to your new school advisor) and you will go far in life.

Happy Feng Shui-ing ...

Recommended Reading

Color-cadabra, Watson-Gupthill Publications, New York, 2004

Dorm Room Feng Shui, Katherine Olaksen, Storey Publishing, North Adams, MA, 2005

Feng Shui Dictionary: Everything you Need to Know to Assess your Space, Find Solutions, and Bring Harmony to your Home, Antonia Beattie, Thunder Bay Press, San Diego, 2003

Feng Shui Step by Step: Arranging your Home for Health and Happiness, T. Raphael Simons, Three Rivers Press, New York, 1996

Funk Shui, Watson-Gupthill Publications, New York, 2004

Teen Feng Shui, Susan Levitt, Bindu Books, Rochester VT, 2003

The Complete Book of Color, Suzy Chiazzari, Barnes and Noble Books, New York, 1998

About the Author

Ms Radaj has a BS in Marketing from Marquette University (with a double minor in psychology and political science—GO MARQUETTE!) and an Interior Design degree from MATC in Milwaukee. Her 15+ years as Operations and Marketing Director for the Nature of Things Stores has led her to numerous design challenges in the development of store spaces of a variety of sizes, custom product development and merchandising strategies. She has been a trainer on the subjects of coaching employees, sales, merchandising and marketing/PR. Ms Radaj has designed retail spaces as well as consulted on numerous residential projects, specializing in bedrooms and nurseries. Ms Radaj is the author of numerous articles, is the former editor of the WI ASID newsletter (which featured her column "The Business of Design" and is still a contributor) and her first design book entitled *Designing the Life of Your Dreams from the Outside In* (7/ 06). Ms Radaj is an avid adventure traveler and is an exhibited nature photographer. She currently resides in Milwaukee (between adventures) with her two dogs that keep her from taking herself too seriously.

978-0-595-42873-1
0-595-42873-8

CPSIA information can be obtained at www.ICGtesting.com
Printed in the USA
BVOW07s1839290914

368788BV00003B/230/P